DATE DUE

AUG 3 0 2006			

DEMCO 38-297

STORY:
ELIZABETH HUDSON-GOFF, KERRI O'HERN,
AND JONATHA A. BROWN

ILLUSTRATIONS:
D. MCHARGUE

WORLD ALMANAC® LIBRARY

FOR MANY YEARS, FARM WORKERS TOILED IN THE HOT SUN. THEY WORKED LONG HOURS DOING HARD LABOR WITH LITTLE PAY. ONE OF THESE FARM WORKERS WAS CÉSAR CHÁVEZ.

CÉSAR CHÁVEZ DID NOT PLAN TO BE A HERO. HE WAS SHY AND HE HAD NO EDUCATION BEYOND THE EIGHTH GRADE. HE DID NOT EVEN SPEAK ENGLISH AS A FIRST LANGUAGE.

BUT CÉSAR WORKED HARD AND EVENTUALLY HELPED MILLIONS OF POOR PEOPLE IMPROVE THEIR LIVES. WITH HIS HELP, FARM WORKERS ORGANIZED TO REDUCE THEIR WORK HOURS, GET BETTER PAY, AND RECEIVE HEALTH CARE.

CÉSAR CHÁVEZ WAS BORN ON MARCH 31, 1927, IN ARIZONA. HE WAS A MEXICAN AMERICAN. HIS GRANDPARENTS HAD COME TO THE UNITED STATES FROM MEXICO IN THE LATE 1800s. THEY BOUGHT LAND IN ARIZONA AND MADE IT INTO A RANCH. THEY GREW CROPS AND RAISED LIVESTOCK.

CÉSAR'S PARENTS HAD FIVE CHILDREN. SOME OF CÉSAR'S AUNTS, UNCLES, AND COUSINS LIVED WITH THEM ON THE FAMILY RANCH. THEY WERE A CLOSE-KNIT, SPANISH-SPEAKING FAMILY.

SOMETIMES CÉSAR WISHED THERE WAS MORE TIME TO PLAY. BUT HE LEARNED HOW TO PLANT SEEDS AND GROW FOOD. HE LEARNED HOW TO WORK TOGETHER WITH OTHERS. ALWAYS, THERE WAS PLENTY OF FOOD AND LOVE TO GO AROUND.

SOMETIMES CÉSAR AND HIS BROTHERS AND SISTERS FOUGHT,

THEIR MOTHER SHOWED THEM HOW TO SOLVE PROBLEMS BY THINKING AND TALKING, NOT FIGHTING. THIS LESSON WAS VERY IMPORTANT TO CÉSAR.

NO RAIN FELL IN ARIZONA FOR MONTHS DURING 1933. CROPS DIED. THE CHÁVEZ FAMILY COULD NOT PAY TAXES ON THEIR LAND.

THE GOVERNMENT TOOK THE FAMILY'S LAND AWAY. SIX-YEAR-OLD CÉSAR WAS CONFUSED AND SCARED. WHERE WOULD THEY GO? HIS MOTHER EXPLAINED THAT THE FAMILY HAD TO LEAVE THEIR HOME.

CÉSAR'S FATHER HOPED TO FIND WORK ON THE HUGE FARMS IN CALIFORNIA. FOR THE NEXT TEN YEARS, THE CHÁVEZ FAMILY WERE MIGRANT WORKERS. MIGRANT WORKERS TRAVELED FROM PLACE TO PLACE LOOKING FOR WORK. SOMETIMES CÉSAR'S SHOES WERE WORN DOWN TO SHREDS FROM WALKING. BUT THERE WAS NO MONEY TO REPLACE THEM.

THE CHÁVEZ FAMILY FOUND WORK ON MANY DIFFERENT KINDS OF FARMS. IN THE FIELDS, THE WHOLE FAMILY TENDED AND PICKED PEAS, CORN, STRAWBERRIES, WALNUTS, MELONS, BEANS, TOMATOES, GRAPES, COTTON, LETTUCE, AND MORE.

THEY WORKED FROM DAWN TO DUSK. THE HAPPY TIMES THAT CÉSAR HAD KNOWN BEFORE WERE GONE. EVERYONE WAS ALWAYS TIRED AND HUNGRY.

WORKING CONDITIONS FOR MIGRANT WORKERS WERE TERRIBLE.

FARMERS COULD PAY THEM ANY AMOUNT THEY WANTED TO. SOMETIMES THE CHÁVEZ FAMILY EARNED ONLY PENNIES A DAY.

EVERYONE IN THE CHÁVEZ FAMILY WORKED. EVEN THE CHILDREN TENDED THE LAND UNDER THE HOT SUN, WITH NO DRINKING WATER OR BATHROOM.

WORKERS COULD NOT AFFORD HEALTH CARE.

THERE WAS VERY LITTLE FOOD. MANY TIMES, THE FAMILY WAS ALMOST STARVING. THEY OFTEN SLEPT UNDER BRIDGES OR IN ABANDONED CARS.

BUT THROUGH ALL OF THESE BAD TIMES, THE FAMILY STAYED TOGETHER. THEY TOOK CARE OF EACH OTHER AS BEST THEY COULD.

CÉSAR MOVED FROM SCHOOL TO SCHOOL DURING THIS TIME. MEXICAN AMERICANS AND MIGRANT WORKERS WERE OFTEN DISCRIMINATED AGAINST. TEACHERS AND OTHER CHILDREN SOMETIMES PICKED ON HIM FOR MAKING MISTAKES IN ENGLISH.

YOU TALK FUNNY!

THEY CALLED CÉSAR "STUPID" BECAUSE HE SPOKE SPANISH. CÉSAR BEGAN TO DREAD GOING TO SCHOOL. HE FELT BAD ABOUT WHO HE WAS.

ONLY HIS PARENTS TOLD HIM HOW IMPORTANT HE WAS. THEY REMINDED HIM EVERY DAY TO HOLD HIS HEAD HIGH.

CÉSAR DROPPED OUT OF SCHOOL IN THE EIGHTH GRADE TO HELP THE FAMILY IN THE FIELDS. IN 1944, DURING WORLD WAR II, CÉSAR JOINED THE NAVY.

HIS JOB, ALONG WITH MOST OTHER MEXICAN AMERICAN SAILORS, WAS TO PAINT THE SHIP AND CLEAN DECKS. HE WAS NOT EVEN ALLOWED TO FIGHT FOR HIS COUNTRY! ONCE AGAIN, CÉSAR HAD TO ENDURE PREJUDICE BECAUSE OF HIS BACKGROUND.

AFTER THE NAVY, CÉSAR RETURNED TO DELANO, CALIFORNIA.

THERE HE FELL IN LOVE WITH A KIND, STRONG WOMAN NAMED HELEN FABELA. THEY MARRIED AND MOVED INTO A ONE-ROOM SHACK.

THEY WERE VERY POOR, BUT THEY HAD EACH OTHER. WITH HOPE IN THEIR HEARTS, THEY STARTED A FAMILY.

NO WORK TODAY

AS POSTED
CITY ORDINANCE
453-JK99
SAL SI PUEDES

BUT THE COUPLE COULD NOT FIND STEADY WORK. FINALLY, CÉSAR MOVED HIS FAMILY TO A VERY POOR TOWN CALLED SAL SI PUEDES. IN ENGLISH, THE NAME MEANS "GET OUT IF YOU CAN." THE NAME FIT.

AL SI
JEDES

SHACKS AND TENTS LINED THE DIRT ROADS. CHILDREN PLAYED IN POLLUTED STREAMS. DISEASES SPREAD EASILY. STARVING DOGS ROAMED THE MUDDY, UNPAVED STREETS. CÉSAR DID NOT WANT THIS LIFE FOR HIS FAMILY—OR FOR ANYONE.

IN 1952, CÉSAR CHÁVEZ MET A CATHOLIC PRIEST NAMED FATHER DONALD MCDONNEL. HE URGED CÉSAR TO READ ABOUT GREAT LEADERS.

HE READ ABOUT THE LIVES OF SAINTS, FREEDOM FIGHTERS, AND LABOR LEADERS.

HE LOVED LEARNING ABOUT GREAT LEADERS LIKE MAHATMA GANDHI.

SOON CÉSAR COULD NOT STOP READING.

THAT SAME YEAR, A MAN NAMED FRED ROSS CAME TO SAL SI PUEDES. ROSS WORKED FOR A GROUP CALLED COMMUNITY SERVICE ORGANIZATION, OR CSO. CSO WORKED TO HELP POOR MEXICAN AMERICANS.

ROSS HAD A LOT OF ENERGY AND IDEAS. HE TOLD CHÁVEZ HOW LABOR UNIONS COULD HELP WORKERS. LABOR UNIONS CAN HELP PROTECT WORKERS. THEY COULD TALK TO COMPANY OWNERS ABOUT WORKERS' NEEDS. THEY COULD ALSO TALK WITH GOVERNMENT OFFICIALS ABOUT WORKERS' NEEDS.

FRED ROSS ALSO SHOWED CÉSAR HOW TO HELP MEXICAN AMERICANS REGISTER TO VOTE. BY VOTING, THEY COULD ELECT POLITICIANS WHO CARED ABOUT THEIR PROBLEMS.

CHÁVEZ SOON BEGAN KNOCKING ON DOORS IN POOR NEIGHBORHOODS.

HE URGED MEXICANS TO APPLY FOR U.S. CITIZENSHIP SO THEY COULD VOTE.

THIS WAS HARD AT FIRST BECAUSE CÉSAR WAS VERY SHY. HE DID NOT KNOW IF PEOPLE WOULD CALL HIM NAMES OR LISTEN TO HIM.

CHÁVEZ BEGAN TO BELIEVE THAT FARM WORKERS DID NOT HAVE TO LIVE IN TERRIBLE CONDITIONS. THEY COULD ORGANIZE AND WORK TOGETHER. POOR PEOPLE COULD CHANGE THEIR OWN LIVES!

IN 1952, THE CSO REGISTERED 6,000 NEW VOTERS IN THE DELANO AREA.

THE GROUP OFFERED CHÁVEZ A FULL-TIME JOB AS AN ORGANIZER. HE WOULD GO TO BIGGER CITIES LIKE OAKLAND AND START NEW CHAPTERS OF THE CSO.

TRUE WEALTH IS NOT MEASURED IN MONEY OR STATUS OR POWER. IT IS MEASURED BY THE LEGACY THAT WE LEAVE BEHIND FOR THOSE WE LOVE AND THOSE WE INSPIRE.

CÉSAR WAS GETTING BETTER AT TALKING TO PEOPLE. MORE AND MORE WORKERS STARTED LISTENING TO HIM. THEY TOLD THEIR FRIENDS. SOON HUNDREDS OF PEOPLE BEGAN TO COME TO HIS MEETINGS.

CÉSAR HAD HIS FIRST BIG SUCCESS IN OXNARD, CALIFORNIA. THERE, HE FOUND THAT LOCAL LABORERS WERE NOT BEING HIRED TO WORK IN THE FIELDS. INSTEAD, GROWERS WERE HIRING ILLEGAL WORKERS CALLED BRACEROS. BRACEROS LIVED IN MEXICO. THE GROWERS BROUGHT THEM TO CALIFORNIA ON BUSES AND PAID THEM VERY LITTLE MONEY TO WORK IN THE FIELDS.

CÉSAR HAD A PLAN TO TELL EVERYONE WHAT THE GROWERS WERE DOING. HE HAD LOCAL WORKERS HOLD SIGNS AROUND TOWN. THE SIGNS SAID THE GROWERS WERE HIRING BRACEROS. THEY WERE NOT GIVING JOBS TO LOCAL WORKERS. CÉSAR ALSO TOLD GOVERNMENT OFFICIALS.

FINALLY THE GROWERS WERE FORCED TO HIRE LOCAL WORKERS INSTEAD OF BRACEROS. HIS PLAN HAD WORKED!

IN 1959, CÉSAR BECAME THE DIRECTOR OF THE CSO. IT WAS THE MOST POWERFUL MEXICAN AMERICAN CIVIL RIGHTS GROUP IN THE UNITED STATES. BUT CÉSAR WANTED TO WORK HARDER FOR FIELD WORKERS IN RURAL AREAS. HE BEGAN A FARM WORKERS' UNION ON HIS OWN. HE CALLED HIS NEW LABOR UNION AN "ASSOCIATION," BECAUSE IT WAS ILLEGAL FOR FARMHANDS TO JOIN A LABOR UNION.

THE ASSOCIATION BEGAN WITH THREE MEMBERS, INCLUDING CÉSAR'S WIFE. THEY TALKED TO THOUSANDS OF CAMPESINOS, OR FIELD WORKERS.

THEY LEARNED ABOUT THE TERRIBLE PROBLEMS THEY FACED EACH DAY. NOT MUCH HAD CHANGED FOR THE WORKERS SINCE CÉSAR WAS A LITTLE BOY.

THE FIGHT IS NEVER ABOUT GRAPES OR LETTUCE. IT IS ABOUT PEOPLE!

AT FIRST, NOT MANY PEOPLE BELIEVED THE GROUP COULD HELP THEM.

BUT CÉSAR WON THE WORKERS OVER. ON SEPTEMBER 20, 1962, THE GROUP HELD ITS FIRST CONVENTION IN FRESNO, CALIFORNIA.

CÉSAR WAS PROUD AND HAPPY. HE WAS NOT PROUD OF HIMSELF BUT OF ALL THE WORKERS WHO STRUGGLED WITH HIM. AND ALWAYS, HE REMEMBERED HIS OWN LIFE IN THE FIELDS.

WORKERS UNITE!!

AT THE MEETING, THEY VOTED TO CALL THEMSELVES THE NATIONAL FARM WORKERS ASSOCIATION, THE NFWA. THE MEMBERS AGREED ON A MOTTO—"VIVA LA CAUSA!" ("LONG LIVE THE CAUSE!"). THEY ALSO APPROVED A DESIGN FOR A NFWA FLAG.

THE NFWA BEGAN SPREADING ITS MESSAGE ACROSS CALIFORNIA. IT PUBLISHED ITS OWN NEWSPAPER. THE PAPER WAS CALLED EL MALCRIADO, MEANING "THE BRAT" OR "THE CHILD WHO SPEAKS BACK TO ITS PARENTS."

CÉSAR WORKED AROUND THE CLOCK. HE ROSE BEFORE DAWN AND WORKED UNTIL WELL AFTER DARK.

MEMBERS ASKED FOR DECENT PAY AND FAIR TREATMENT. THEY CALLED FOR FARM LABORERS TO WORK TOGETHER FOR CHANGE.

IN 1965, A GROUP OF FILIPINO WORKERS AND THE NFWA GOT TOGETHER. LOCAL GRAPE GROWERS WERE TREATING THE FILIPINOS UNFAIRLY.

THE TWO GROUPS HELD A STRIKE AGAINST 48 RANCHES. THEY REFUSED TO WORK. THE GREAT DELANO GRAPE STRIKE HAD BEGUN.

THE STRIKING WORKERS STOOD OUTSIDE THE RANCHES. THEY HELD SIGNS THAT ASKED PEOPLE NOT TO BUY FOOD FROM THESE RANCHES.

I DON'T LIKE YOU!

RANCHERS AND HOSTILE POLICEMEN YELLED AT THE STRIKERS AND EVEN PUSHED AND BEAT THEM.

KEEP OUT OF THIS FATHER! THIS IS NONE OF YOUR BUSINESS!

CÉSAR HAD PRIESTS AND MINISTERS JOIN THE STRIKERS. THEY REMINDED WORKERS TO STAY CALM. THANKS TO CÉSAR'S EFFORTS, THE STRIKERS DID NOT PHYSICALLY FIGHT BACK.

ON MARCH 17, 1966, CÉSAR AND OTHER NFWA SUPPORTERS BEGAN A 350-MILE (565-KILOMETER) WALK FROM DELANO TO THE STATE CAPITAL IN SACRAMENTO. THEY WANTED TO TALK TO THE GOVERNOR.

FINALLY, A UNION WAS FORMED CALLED THE UNITED FARM WORKERS ORGANIZING COMMITTEE, OR THE UFWOC. CÉSAR WAS ELECTED ITS DIRECTOR. HE CONTINUED WITH THE STRIKES AND BOYCOTTS. THE STRIKES GOT MORE VIOLENT. GROWERS BEAT UP STRIKERS. WORKERS GOT DISCOURAGED, EVEN SCARED. THERE SEEMED TO BE NO END.

EQUAL RIGHTS FOR FARM WORKERS!

MEANWHILE, CÉSAR AND HIS FAMILY REMAINED POOR. CÉSAR NEVER WANTED HIS PERSONAL FORTUNES TO RISE ABOVE THE WORKERS HE WAS FIGHTING FOR.

CÉSAR WANTED TO ENCOURAGE HIS WORKERS. HE DECIDED TO SHOW THEM HOW STRONGLY HE FELT ABOUT THEIR CAUSE. HE STOPPED EATING ON FEBRUARY 15, 1968. BY REFUSING FOOD, CÉSAR HOPED TO SHOW HIS COMMITMENT TO NONVIOLENCE. DAYS PASSED, AND STILL CÉSAR ATE NO FOOD.

HIS HUNGER STRIKE LASTED FOR MORE THAN THREE WEEKS. THE NEWS MEDIA REPORTED CÉSAR'S STRIKE. AMERICANS BEGAN TO CARE ABOUT THE FIELD WORKERS.

DOCK WORKERS REFUSED TO UNLOAD AMERICAN GRAPES. AMERICANS STOPPED BUYING GRAPES AT THE GROCERY STORES.

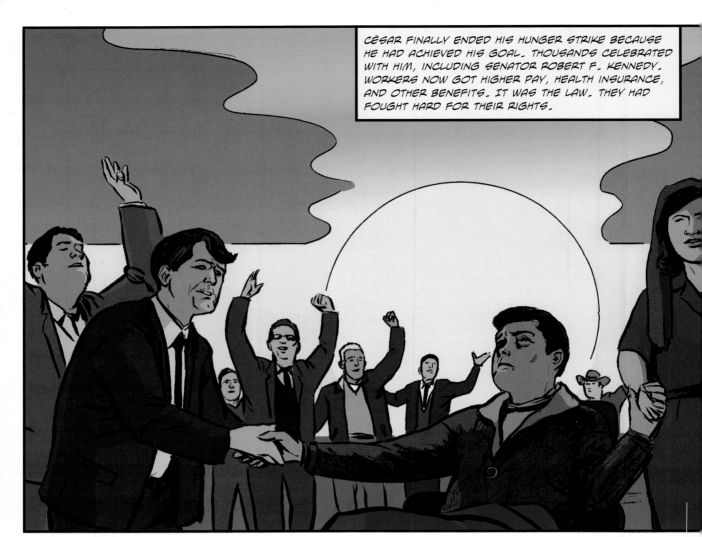

CÉSAR FINALLY ENDED HIS HUNGER STRIKE BECAUSE HE HAD ACHIEVED HIS GOAL. THOUSANDS CELEBRATED WITH HIM, INCLUDING SENATOR ROBERT F. KENNEDY. WORKERS NOW GOT HIGHER PAY, HEALTH INSURANCE, AND OTHER BENEFITS. IT WAS THE LAW. THEY HAD FOUGHT HARD FOR THEIR RIGHTS.

CÉSAR NEVER WAVERED FROM HIS GOALS. HE ALWAYS BELIEVED EVERYONE SHOULD HAVE EQUAL OPPORTUNITY FOR EDUCATION, HEALTH CARE, AND DECENT PAY. EVERYONE SHOULD BE TREATED WITH DIGNITY AS A HUMAN BEING.

IN 1988, CHÁVEZ BEGAN ANOTHER HUNGER STRIKE. THIS TIME HE WANTED GROWERS TO STOP USING HARMFUL CHEMICALS ON PLANTS. THE CHEMICALS POISONED MANY FARM WORKERS.

CÉSAR CHÁVEZ DIED IN HIS SLEEP ON APRIL 23, 1993. HE WAS SIXTY-SIX YEARS OLD. IN ALL THOSE YEARS, HE NEVER OWNED A HOUSE OR A CAR. HIS WORK FOR JUSTICE WAS HIS PASSION HIS WHOLE LIFE.

IN 1994, PRESIDENT BILL CLINTON AWARDED THE PRESIDENTIAL MEDAL OF FREEDOM TO CÉSAR CHÁVEZ. HELEN CHÁVEZ ACCEPTED THE MEDAL IN HER HUSBAND'S PLACE.

"BECAUSE WE HAVE SUFFERED, AND WE ARE NOT AFRAID TO SUFFER IN ORDER TO SURVIVE, WE ARE READY TO GIVE UP EVERYTHING—EVEN OUR LIVES—IN OUR STRUGGLE FOR JUSTICE."

—CÉSAR CHÁVEZ
SEPTEMBER 16, 1965

MORE BOOKS TO READ

César Chávez. Susan Zannos (Mitchell Lane Publishers)

César Chávez: Leader for Migrant Farm Workers. Hispanic Biographies (series). Doreen Gonzales (Enslow Publishers)

César Chávez. Just the Facts Biographies (series). David R. Collins (Lerner Publications)

César Chávez: A Hero for Everyone. Milestone (series). Gary Soto (Simon & Schuster Children's Publishing)

César Chávez. Trailblazers of the Modern World (series). Jonatha A. Brown (World Almanac Library)

Remembering César: The Legacy of César Chávez. Ann McGregor (Quill Driver Books)

WEB SITES

César Chávez and the Farmworkers' Struggle
www.pbs.org/itvs/fightfields

The César E. Chávez Foundation Site
www.cesarechavezfoundation.org/Default.aspx?pi=33

Freedom Heroes
myhero.com/myhero/hero.asp?hero=c_chavez

Library of Congress, Activists & Reformers, César Chávez
www.americaslibrary.gov/cgi-bin/page.cgi/aa/activists/chavez

United Farm Workers History
www.ufw.org/history.htm

Please visit our web site at: www.worldalmanaclibrary.com
For a free color catalog describing World Almanac® Library's list of high-quality books and multimedia programs, call 1-800-848-2928 (USA) or 1-800-387-3178 (Canada). World Almanac® Library's fax: (414) 332-3567.

Library of Congress Cataloging-in-Publication Data

Hudson-Goff, Elizabeth.
   César Chávez / Elizabeth Hudson-Goff, Kerri O'Hern and Jonatha A. Brown.
     p. cm. — (Graphic biographies)
     ISBN 0-8368-6195-7 (lib. bdg.)
     ISBN 0-8368-6247-3 (softcover)
     1. Chavez, Cesar, 1927-1993. Labor leaders—United States—Biography.
3. Mexican Americans—Biography. 4. Agricultural laborers—Labor unions—United States—History—20th century. I. O'Hern, Kerri. II. Brown, Jonatha A. III. Title. IV. Graphic biographies.
HD6509.C48G64   2006
331.88'13092—dc22
                       2005027737

First published in 2006 by
World Almanac® Library
A Member of the WRC Media Family of Companies
330 West Olive Street, Suite 100
Milwaukee, WI 53212 USA

Copyright © 2006 by World Almanac® Library.

Produced by Design Press, a division of the Savannah College of Art and Design
Design: Janice Shay and Maria Angela Rojas
Editing: Kerri O'Hern and Elizabeth Hudson-Goff
Illustration: D. McHargue
World Almanac® Library editorial direction: Mark Sachner and Valerie J. Weber
World Almanac® Library art direction: Tammy West

Printed in the United States of America

1 2 3 4 5 6 7 8 9 10 09 08 07 06